Spotlight on
Kids Can Code

What Are
INTEGRATED CIRCUITS?

Patricia Harris

PowerKiDS press
New York

Published in 2018 by The Rosen Publishing Group, Inc.
29 East 21st Street, New York, NY 10010

Copyright © 2018 by The Rosen Publishing Group, Inc.

All rights reserved. No part of this book may be reproduced in any form without permission in writing from the publisher, except by a reviewer.

First Edition

Editor: Theresa Morlock
Book Design: Michael J. Flynn

Photo Credits: Cover Hero Images/Hero Images/Getty Images;
p. 5 (top) Rawpixel.com/Shutterstock.com; p. 5 (bottom) Karynav/Shutterstock.com;
p. 7 (transistor) a_v_d/Shutterstock.com; p. 7 (diode) Sergio Delle Vedove/Shutterstock.com;
p. 7 (resistor) niwat chaiyawoot/Shutterstock.com; p. 7 (capacitor) Danny Iacob/Shutterstock.com;
p. 7 (computer) Ti Santi/Shutterstock.com; p. 8 David Silverman/Getty Images News/Getty Images;
p. 9 https://commons.wikimedia.org/wiki/File:GeoffreyDummer.jpg; p. 11 (calculator) Claudio Divizia/Shutterstock.com; p. 11 (microchip) Andrew Burton/Getty Images News/Getty Images;
p. 13 (circuit board) alessen/Shutterstock.com; p. 13 (computer chip) MirageC/Moment/Getty Images;
p. 15 Bill Varie/Corbis/Getty Images; p. 16 Michael Staniewski/Shutterstock.com;
p. 17 franz12/Shutterstock.com; p. 18 Fekete Tibor/Shutterstock.com; p. 19 Justin Sullivan/Getty Images News/Getty Images; p. 21 science photo/Shutterstock.com.

Cataloging-in-Publication Data

Names: Harris, Patricia.
Title: What are integrated circuits? / Patricia Harris.
Description: New York : PowerKids Press, 2018. | Series: Spotlight on kids can code | Includes index.
Identifiers: ISBN 9781508155300 (pbk.) | ISBN 9781508155195 (library bound) | ISBN 9781508154846 (6 pack)
Subjects: LCSH: Integrated circuits–Juvenile literature. | Integrated circuits–History–Juvenile literature.
Classification: LCC TK7820.H37 2018 | DDC 621.3815–dc23

Manufactured in the United States of America

CPSIA Compliance Information: Batch #BS17PK: For Further Information contact Rosen Publishing, New York, New York at 1-800-237-9932

Contents

Computer Technology in Daily Life.....4
Before Integrated Circuits............6
The Idea Is Born.....................8
Integrated Circuits in the
     United States 10
What's an Integrated Circuit?........12
Designing Integrated Circuits........14
Fabrication..........................16
Moore's Law..........................18
What's to Come?......................20
New Advances.........................22
Glossary.............................23
Index................................24
Websites.............................24

Computer Technology in Daily Life

Many people today use several forms of computer **technology** in their daily lives. For example, a student might have a tablet on their desk so they can complete a math test and have it scored as soon as they've finished. They might also have a smartphone in their pocket. The student might also be wearing a watch that's connected to their smartphone so they can **access** information while walking in the halls or eating lunch.

All of this connectivity is possible because computerized devices have integrated circuits. An integrated circuit is an electronic circuit that's built onto a small, hard surface of **semiconducting** material. Integrated circuits are sometimes called chips or microchips. Without integrated circuits and new advances in circuit design, powerful and small devices like tablets, smartphones, and smartwatches wouldn't be possible.

Integrated circuits make it possible for technology to be **portable**.

5

Before Integrated Circuits

The first computers filled whole rooms with mechanical switches. Later, vacuum tubes were used to **transmit** information in computers. Computers were housed in special rooms to keep them cool and provide space for all the **components**.

In the 1950s, scientists began to use **transistors** in computers. However, computers that used transistors were still very large. Each transistor had to be connected to other components with wires. The electric signals had to pass through all this wire. The speed of the computer depended on the length of the wires linking the components. All the connections between individual items on a circuit board meant that computers sometimes had problems with connections failing.

transistor
A semiconductor device with three connections.

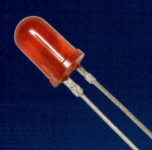

diode
A semiconductor device with two connections.

resistor
A device designed to resist, or block, the passing of an electric current.

> Over time, computers and other devices have changed. Computers have become smaller, slimmer, and more efficient.

capacitor
A device used to store an electrical charge.

7

The Idea Is Born

In the 1950s, computer scientists began to think about how to improve a computer's reliability, size, and speed. A British engineer named Geoffrey Dummer was the first person to suggest the idea of integrated circuits.

Dummer proposed that the transistors and connections that were then included on circuit boards could all be made in a solid block. He said that the block could contain layers of transistors, **amplifying** components, conductors, and insulators. He said that the layers of the block could be cut away to make connections. In the late 1950s, Dummer made a model from a block of silicon (an element) with four transistors, insulators, and connectors. Unfortunately, the idea didn't take off right away.

Over his lifetime, Dummer received several awards and honors for his electrical engineering work.

Integrated Circuits in the United States

In the late 1950s and early 1960s, two men working for different companies in the United States had ideas much like Dummer's. The two men were Jack Kilby, who worked for a company called Texas Instruments, and Robert Noyce, who worked for his own company called Fairchild Semiconductor. Kilby and Noyce both proposed that silicon blocks could be used to make all parts of a circuit.

Silicon was already used to make some transistors, but Kilby decided that diodes, resistors, and capacitors could also be made from silicon. Both companies were given **patents** for the idea. By the late 1960s, creating and using integrated circuit chips was a big business. Integrated circuits made a difference in the size and speed of electronic devices.

electronic calculator 1976

In 1967, Texas Instruments created the first handheld electronic calculator. Handheld electronic calculators contain integrated circuits.

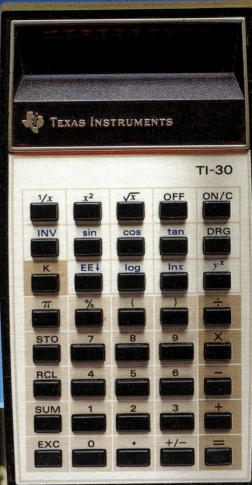

This is the model of the microchip that was created by Jack Kilby.

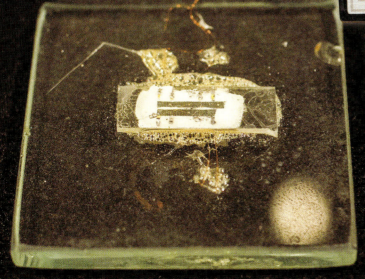

What's an Integrated Circuit?

What was this integrated circuit that was quickly changing the computer industry? It was exactly what Dummer proposed: an electrical circuit including transistors and other components, all made out of a very small block of semiconducting material, usually silicon. Here is a picture of a circuit board with transistors, diodes, resistors, and capacitors all connected with wires. The wires are not visible because they are on the underside of the board, but you can see the connectors going through holes in the board.

Now think of these components in an integrated circuit. Here is an integrated circuit placed on a fingertip. You can see why integrated circuits changed technology. We have moved from boards, with individual components that had to be carefully connected, to single blocks that contain all the components and the connectors.

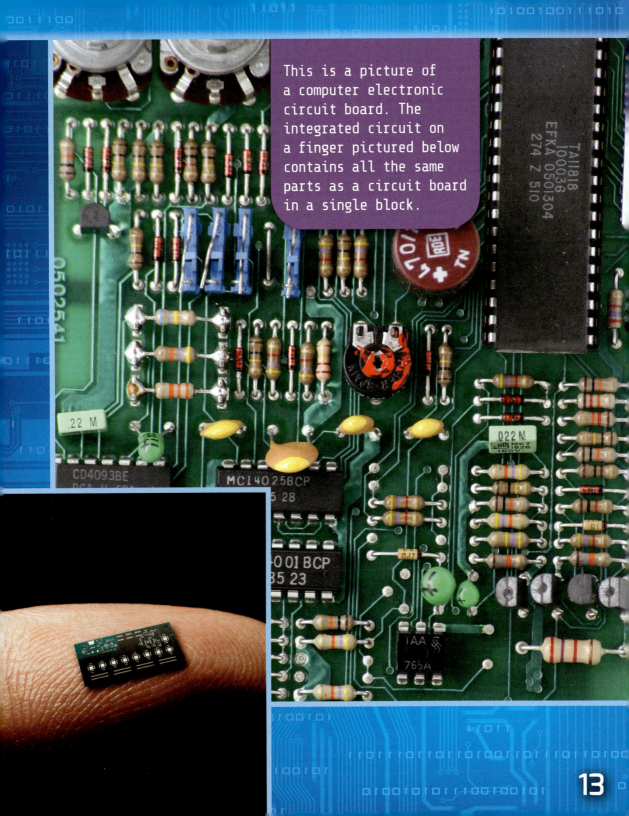

This is a picture of a computer electronic circuit board. The integrated circuit on a finger pictured below contains all the same parts as a circuit board in a single block.

13

Designing Integrated Circuits

Integrated circuits can perform many different functions. They can be used to make timers, counters, amplifiers, computer memory, and microprocessors. What an integrated circuit chip does depends on the design of the circuit.

The design process for microchips has many steps. Computer-assisted design (CAD) supports the work at every step of the process. The first steps focus on what the chip should do, the overall design of the circuit, and the **logic** design needed by the circuit. The next steps focus on the physical design of the system and testing that design. Next, the design is used to create **photomasks**. Work then moves from the design stage to the **fabrication** stage.

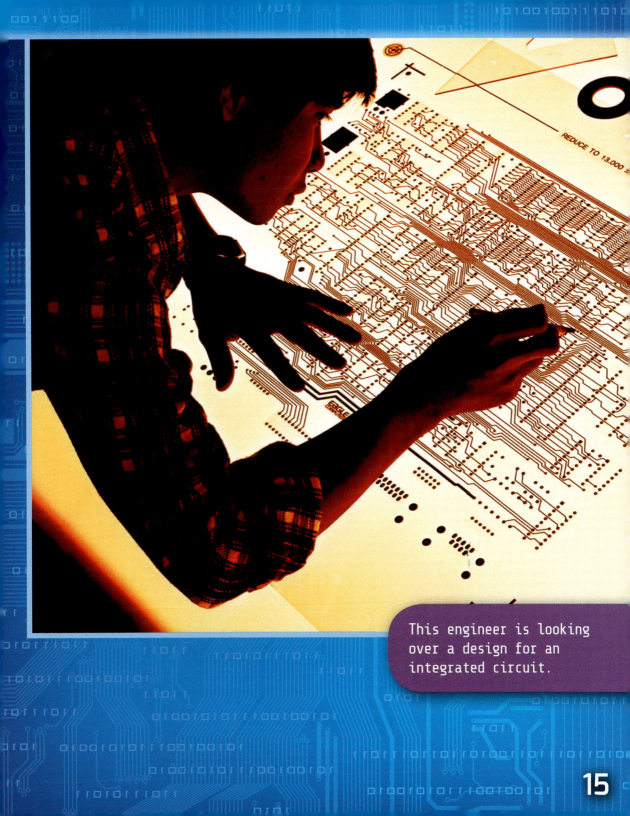

This engineer is looking over a design for an integrated circuit.

Fabrication

The fabrication stage includes the creation of very pure, polished silicon wafers. Silica, also known as silicon dioxide (SiO$_2$), is a major part of sand. Silica exists in nature as a rock called quartz. The silica taken from quartz is used to make microchips. Silica is converted to pure silicon, which is cut into wafers. The wafers are then cleaned and polished. The wafers are used with photomasks in a process to transfer the pattern of the mask to the surface of the wafer. There are many steps to using masks, with special steps in between to separate the parts.

A finished wafer can be cut into many pieces, each with the desired properties. These are microchips. After testing, microchips are packaged in ceramic coverings with appropriate connectors.

silicon wafer

Microchips are produced in factories using machines that can create parts much smaller than ones that could be made by hand.

Moore's Law

A man named Gordon Moore forecast the future of integrated circuits. Moore was the director of research and development for Fairchild Semiconductors. Using data from 1959 to 1964, Moore said in 1965 that the number of components that could be included in an integrated circuit would double every year for 20 years. By 1975, the data showed that he was right!

Advances came from changes in the processes used to produce silicon wafers and integrated circuits. More components could be included on each chip because computer engineers worked to produce better circuit designs and better layouts for the components. The challenge of what came to be known as "Moore's law" led to advances in the science of production and the art of designing integrated circuits.

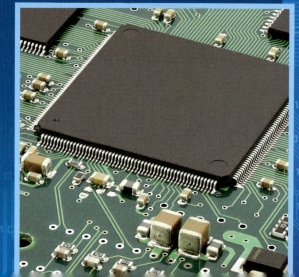

Gordon Moore co-founded the Intel Corporation, a successful technology company.

What's to Come?

In 1975, Moore said that the number of components would double every two years instead of one. Engineers have worked hard to meet that challenge. Today, however, the rate of growth has slowed and Moore's law may no longer hold true.

The growth rate continued for some time because components in integrated circuits have gotten smaller. Now, some people think transistors often used in integrated circuits can't be made any smaller. Even if integrated circuits can be smaller, some manufacturers feel that it won't be cost-effective to make them that small. Integrated circuits today are very cost-effective. However, new materials and new structures within integrated circuits may make it possible for them to continue to become smaller.

> What do you think integrated circuits might look like in the future?

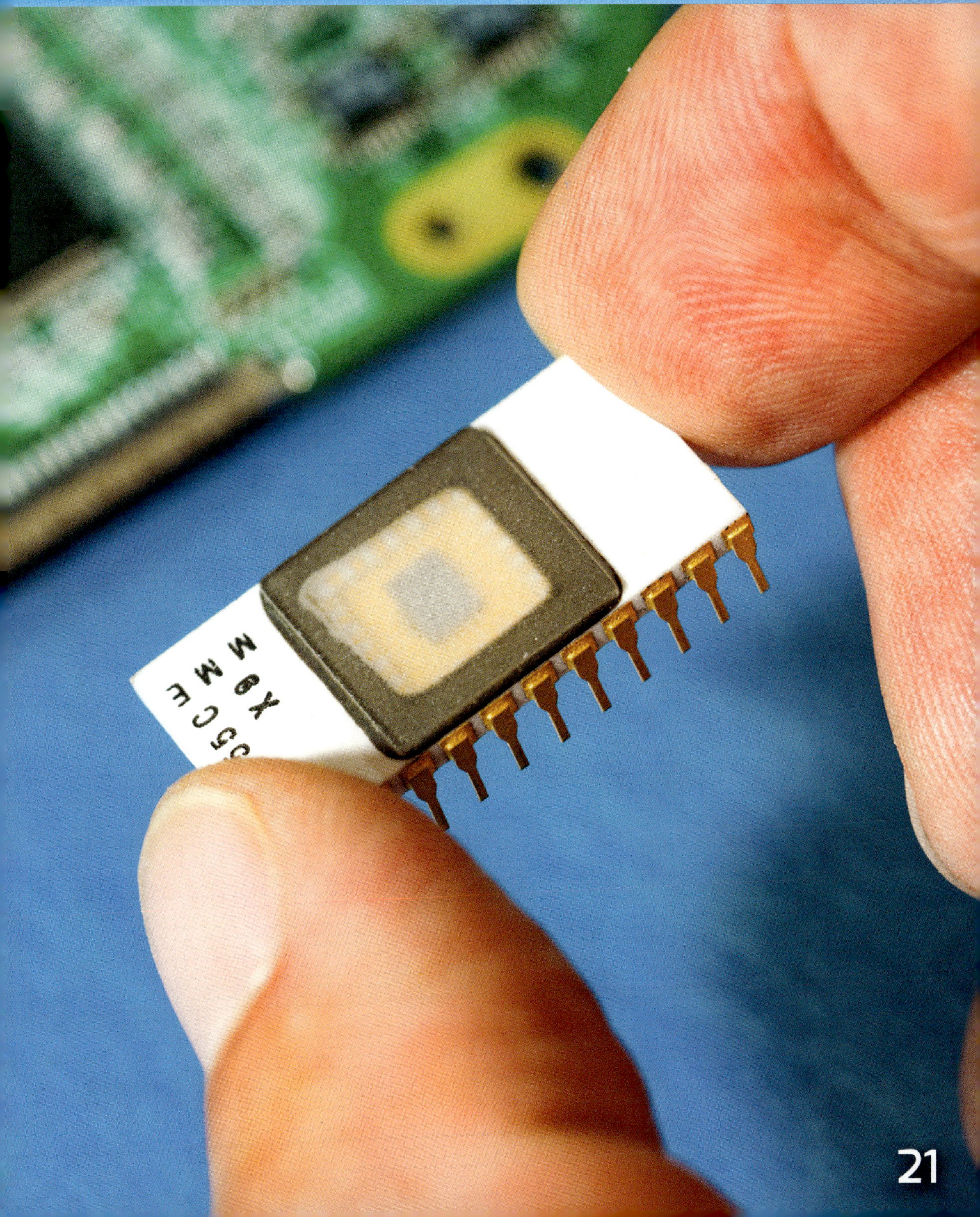

New Advances

A new design idea called 3-D packaging suggests that each small chip can be stacked onto others before the chips are packaged. Stacking the chips means less space is needed. Also, scientists are developing new, faster semiconductors.

Another idea called spintronics is being used to reach higher computing speeds. Spintronics uses the spin of individual electrons in graphene to **encode** data. Graphene is a thin layer of pure carbon formed with one layer of carbon atoms tightly packed together. Also, the transistors used in integrated circuits are being redesigned using metals instead of silicon.

As new advances in integrated circuits are made, the technology we use in our daily lives will continue to change. When the first computers were made, few people could imagine that someday ordinary people would be able to carry computer technology in their pockets. However, integrated circuits made this possible. We may continue to be surprised by what the future of computer technology has in store.

Glossary

access: The ability to use or enter something.

amplify: To increase the strength or amount of something.

component: One of the important parts of something.

encode: To convert information into a coded form.

fabrication: The process of constructing something out of parts.

logic: The steps of thought used to solve or understand a problem.

patent: A document that grants the right from the government to make, use, or sell an invention.

photomask: A photographic pattern used in making microcircuits.

portable: Able to be carried or moved around.

semiconducting: Having the ability to conduct or transfer electricity under certain circumstances.

technology: Industry that deals with electronics and computers.

transistor: A device used to control the flow of electricity in computers and other electronic devices.

transmit: To pass something from one thing to another.

Index

C
capacitor, 7, 10, 12
circuit board, 6, 8, 12, 13
computer-assisted design, 14
conductors, 8

D
diodes, 7, 10, 12
Dummer, Geoffrey, 8, 9, 10, 12

E
electrons, 22

F
Fairchild Semiconductor, 10, 18

G
graphene, 22

I
insulators, 8
Intel Corporation, 19

K
Kilby, Jack, 10, 11

M
Moore, Gordon, 18, 19, 20
Moore's law, 18, 20

N
Noyce, Robert, 10

P
photomasks, 14, 16

R
resistors, 7, 10, 12

S
silica (silicon dioxide), 16
silicon, 8, 10, 12, 16, 18, 22
spintronics, 22

T
Texas Instruments, 10, 11
3-D packaging, 22
transistors, 6, 7, 8, 10, 12, 20, 22

U
United States, 10

V
vacuum tubes, 6

W
wires, 6, 12

Websites

Due to the changing nature of Internet links, PowerKids Press has developed an online list of websites related to the subject of this book. This site is updated regularly. Please use this link to access the list: www.powerkidslinks.com/skcc/circ